From the Issues of My Heart, I Speak

Sharon Session

ISBN-13: 978-1735445700

DEDICATION

To my heart –
you've stuck with me all my life and
you always told the truth
even when I didn't want to listen.

To those who hold a place in my heart –
I pray you forever feel
as treasured as you are.

Sight is a function of the eyes,
Vision is a function of the heart.
- Dr. Myles Munroe

I am grateful for the vision to see the things
reality had yet to. . . and the heart to go chase them.

Contents –

In acknowledgment of the heart   - page 7

Heart's issue: **heard**   - page 11
    Poem title: *The Bridge*

Heart's issue: **safeguarded**   - page 15
    Poem title: *My Eyes Also Watch God*

Heart's issue: **exasperated**   - page 19
    Poem title: *Conjunctions and Contingencies*

Heart's issue: **uncertain**   - page 21
    Poem title: *Going Against the Wind*

Heart's issue: **unobstructed**   - page 25
    Poem title: *The Invitation*

Heart's issue: **transformed**   - page 29
    Poem title: *One Word Can Change Your Whole World*

Heart's issue: **hesitant**   - page 31
    Poem title: *Sentence Fragments.*

Heart's issue: **evolved**   - page 35
    Poem title: *The Constant Metamorphosis*

Heart's issue: **insignificant**   - page 37
    Poem title: *Look Again (Men As Trees Walking)*

Heart's issue: **staccato**   - page 41
    Poem title: *Stutter.*

Heart's issue: **re-defined**   - page 47
    Poem title: *Be Still (Psalm 42)*

Heart's issue: **educated**   - page 51
    Poem title: *Increase My Vocabulary*

Heart's issue: **adventurous**   - page 55
    Poem title: *Well Wishes*

Heart's issue: **paused**   - page 59
    Poem title: *The Narrative*

Heart's issue: **manufactured**   - page 61
    Poem title: *The Mosaic*

Heart's issue: **regret**   - page 65
    Poem title: *The Change Within the Cocoon*

Heart's issue: **foolish**   - page 67
    Poem title: *Untitled (Inside Love)*

Heart's issue: **unashamed**   - page 69
    Poem title: *The Precipice*

Heart's issue: **contaminated**   - page 73
    Poem title: *Live Love, Live*

Heart's issue: **disenfranchised**   - page 77
    Poem title: *Out of Character*

Heart's issue: **liberated**   - page 79
    Poem title: *I Speak*

About the Author   - page 83

In ACKNOWLEDGMENT of the heart. . .

Examine the clover – Have you ever noticed how perfectly-heart shaped each leaf is, and how, even if it's just 3 leaves, it's still lucky because it's . . .

Love.

All of nature, one way or another, operates on love. And what is the universal symbol for love - - - the heart.

The heart is an amazingly powerful thing. In medical terms, it is generally the size of a person's fist, yet it is responsible for pumping blood through every vein within that person's body for the entire day of every day of that person's life. Even though the heart is a function of the body, there are many things the mind can do that has the ability to strain the heart! Mental issues, such as depression, can greatly increase the likelihood of things that attack the heart and weaken its ability to function.

Why is that?

While the heart may physically carry our blood, it metaphorically carries our hopes and dreams.

If your heart and the mind are not aligned, neither can the rest of the body and the rest of life align with you. Don't let life's issues sever your alignment. If it succeeds, those issues plot to assassinate your spirit, your dreams, and your will to survive. In short, it plots to annihilate . . . your heart.

So, keep listening to your heart – it's fighting for your survival.

Not because it's selfish, but because it knows - not only can it NOT live without you, but you cannot live without it.

Without your heart, you cannot live.
(and I mean that in more ways than just one. . .)

Keep thy heart with all diligence
(above all else guard your heart);
for out of it are the issues of life . . .
Proverbs 4:23

From the Issues of My Heart, I Speak

Things that make the **heart feel heard**:

Knowing it's not alone on this journey –

because now,
after reading someone else's words,
      hearing someone else's thoughts, and
      seeing someone else's life,

it knows that
someone else understands
at least a portion of the journey it's on –

and finds comfort in that knowledge.

May you and your heart enjoy the journey together.

The Bridge

I stand in the middle
    in the present.
    in the right now.

On one side is the past,
on the other side is the future,
and I am standing – stuck – in between.

Between desire and destiny
Between peril and promise
Between beneath and beyond

And I'm standing in the middle
    with a choice.

Do I move forward or backward?
    forward to the unknown, or
    backward to the wish-I-could-forget?

Because right now I'm just standing,
    frozen in the middle.

But I can't stand here for long
because even though I don't know what to choose –
I know not making a choice is not an option.

So I choose forward.

I choose forward because
Destiny is greater than desire.
Promise is safer than peril.
Beyond is higher than beneath.

So I choose forward
because I was afraid to turn around
to the past
and become the pillar of salt.
I've known too many salty people
and the doctor says too much salt can
cause high blood pressure,
which could lead to early and unusual death.
Ask Lot's wife.

So I choose forward
because God stands there,
at that end of the bridge,
drawing me nearer
and He is not on the side of my past.

I got stuck in the middle because,
Like the disciples,
I got out of the boat,
and started to walk
but along the way,
lost focus and became afraid -

and paralyzed.

So,
I was standing on a bridge,

I was stuck in the middle,
I was unsure of what to do –

but now,

I am choosing to move forward.
I am choosing to look ahead.
I am choosing to come closer to the spot
in which, I know, God stands.
I am choosing to refocus and press toward the prize.

Because along the path of this bridge
I've passed too many dreams
That have fallen down and died.

Now there's a resurrection of all that lives inside.
So now, away from this bridge,
is where my hope resides.

I'm no longer standing in the middle,
I'm pressing on instead –
Allowing faith to guide and replace fear
I'm not looking back,

but ahead.

Things that make the **heart feel safeguarded**:

Knowing the question isn't
"what would it do if it knew it would not fail"

because there is security in knowing that –
even if it fails –

       and falls –

It still falls in God. . .

because God is everywhere.

My Eyes Also Watch God

My eyes are watching God
Because His eyes are watching me;
I know that I'm the creation
That He loves, the most, to see.

And it's not with vain assurance
That I say this to be true –
It's because every morning He shows me,
And tells me "I love you."

I was standing outside one morning
In a field of purples and green;
The white puffs were covering blue skies
and God couldn't clearly see me.

So he caused a wind to blow,
and right above my head –
Those white puffs did go,
and then there was no dread.

Because when I looked up,
He looked down,
and it was only me to see.

Then I smiled up,
and he smiled down,
and a butterfly flew past me.

(You see, the butterfly is our secret symbol
When one flies past, I do
Know whatever I am thinking
God agrees with me is true.)

And at that moment, I was thinking
I'm grateful to have a God that loves me true –
and then, the butterfly, it confirmed to me,
Yes child, I love you too.

You see, my eyes are watching you
because your eyes are watching me;
You are my creation
and with your heart, I long to be.

So keep standing still in your fields of green,
Or in your driveway too –
And when you look up and see clouds are moving,
Know I'm just getting a good look at you.

In Memory of Jimmie Lee Murray

On one side is the past,
on the other side is the future,
and I am standing
stuck
in between

…

I am choosing to move forward.

"The Bridge"

From the Issues of My Heart, I Speak.

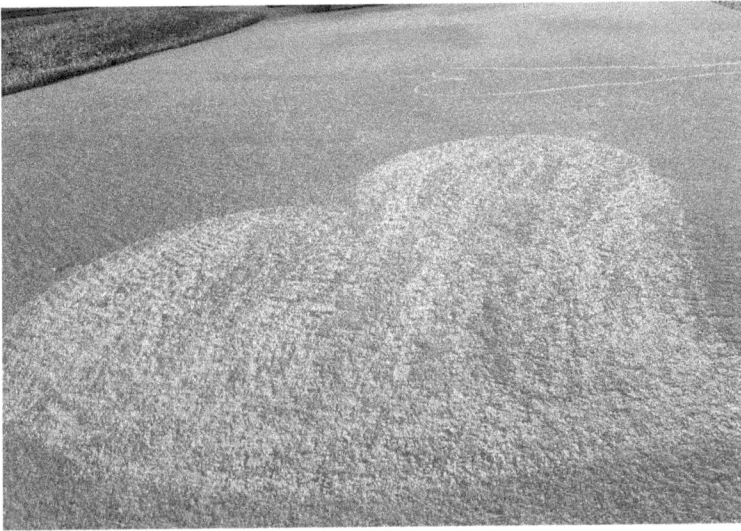

Things that make the **heart feel exasperated:**

Knowing that the
only thing
it needs

to save its private universe

is love,

and even though
the heart
is
the very symbol

of love,

it can't find it.

Conjunctions and Contingencies

I wonder what it would be like to wake up in Paris
- or anyplace other than this.
Lately I've been waking up in disappointment…
- and the rent has become too high.

- but anything that costs any piece of one's soul is,
of course, priced too high.

- But….
If where love is, there is God
because God is love,
then where is God
if I don't love myself?

He's still there,
- and He's waiting.

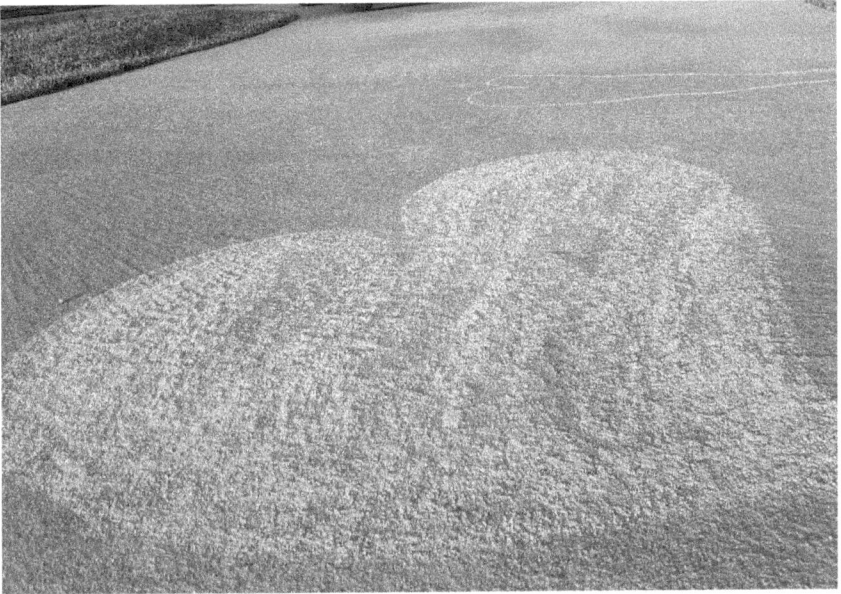

Things that make the **heart feel uncertain:**

Knowing it is now full where it didn't know it was empty

and then He came . . .

Knowing it was addicted to the synthetic and then it met the real

and then He came . . .

Knowing that once it met the real, it had no choice but to want more (and then the addiction became really real)
-

Because, He came . . .

Selah.

Going Against the Wind

Sometimes trying to fall in love
- - - again

It feels like a butterfly
going in the opposite direction,
flapping against a strong wind
          - or even against a breeze.

It seems

aerodynamically impossible
physically improbable
and even
morally irresponsible.

Yet,
there it is.

It's a work.

It weighs upon the already strained heart,
Presses upon the memories of the mind
And it seeks to tear the world, as you know it, apart –
          leaving only shreds behind.

But, yet, there it is –
          This possibility of improbability.

But they say a butterfly can flap its wings

And create a storm that's many miles away.

So –
if this butterfly can cause the wind
     And then flap against its flow,

Then, maybe,
     Re-falling in love won't be so bad,
     Who knows where these winds may blow?

But, certainly, I think I'd like to know. . .

love
doesn't equal
life
until it inspires
the best parts of you

"Stutter."

From the Issues of My Heart, I Speak

Things that make the **heart feel unobstructed**:

Knowing that it is free to do and desires to do

exactly that

which it was asked to do . . .

Just come.

The Invitation

I got invited to something today.
Not anything I hadn't been invited to before.
In fact, I've received this invitation
many times before,
at many different places.

It's not an unusual invitation.
It's an invitation that's been extended for years.
Decades even.
Centuries!

I just finally accepted it.
For myself.
For real this time.

It's not an invitation that comes in a fancy envelope
     Written in fancy penmanship and
        Delivered with fancy stamps by the mailman.

It's not an invitation that dings in your inbox,
     attaching you to your computer,
   requesting that you click to open,
    and tells you it's awaiting your clicked response.

It just asks –
Yes? No? Maybe?

But it is an invitation
     That starts in the heart

That's spoken through a mouth
That's extended through a hand
And says "come."

That's all.
"Come."

No dress code required.
No presents required.
No inconvenience required.

Just come.

And it's the best invitation ever.
And it's one I'll never regret accepting.

There will be no love dying here —

It won't need a band-aid
nor stitches,
No tourniquets,
nor gauze
. . .
No one will need to call
the time of death
nor the next of kin.

"Live Love, Live"

From the Issues of My Heart, I Speak

Things that make the **heart feel transformed:**

Knowing that what it
was
is no longer what it
is - - -

and it **can still** smile.

It can smile because that statement was true
yesterday,
today,
and it will, again, be true
tomorrow.

One Word Can Change Your Whole World

Life

will

make

you

learn

that

time

truly

does

bring

about

change.

Things that make the **heart feel hesitant:**

Knowing that
it's the

invisible things

that are
the
hardest to fight –

things

like

feelings.

Sentence Fragments.

I've always told you the truth.
I just put periods.
where they didn't necessarily belong.

Truth is still truth even if it's fragmented.

The truth is —
The whole truth is —
I was afraid to tell you the whole truth.

Afraid to say
"I think I'm falling in love with you"
In case "I just like you" was the feeling in return.
or worse -
"I admire you."
Because you never fall in love with the people you admire.
You know, like you admire your grandma.
You admire the strength of your grandma.
You admire the courage of Martin Luther King.
You admire the creativity of, I don't know, Benjamin
    Franklin, or Michael Jackson, Salvador Dali or
    someone like that.

But the phrase you never say after you say
"I admire them" is
"I hope to marry them one day."
(Although I did used to want to marry Michael
Jackson – but I was 6 at the time).

Not that I want to marry you, but. . .
I'd at least like to. . .
go the to the movies?
maybe have dinner?
maybe cook dinner together?
…..but not today!

Sometime after admire turns to like
and like turns to love
and love turns to
I never want to not have you in my life.

Because the truth is. . .
The whole truth is –
My heart is precious to me.
And over time of giving it to people,
people who ultimately and eventually
treated it like it was yesterday's leftovers –
they'd pick out what they want and throw the rest in
the trash
or worse – feed it to the dogs.

I've finally discovered its worth.
In doing so, I've also discovered my own.

And I'm worth more.
Than to be just admired.
Than to be loved distantly like grandma, or
Martin Luther King, or Benjamin Franklin,
Michael Jackson or Salvador Dali.

I'm worthy of being loved like me.
So the truth is. . .
I mean the whole truth.
And not a fragment of the truth.
Is that I finally love me. A lot.
But,
I need someone who loves me more.
than just a fragment.

Things that make the **heart feel evolved:**

When it can thank God

not only for –

Who God is,
When God is, and
How God is . . .

But the heart can also thank God for

who it is
and
who it is becoming.

The Constant Metamorphosis

I've changed.
But I was supposed to change.
I went into my cocoon to change.
The purpose of a cocoon is to change.

The caterpillar doesn't go inside its cocoon until it's ready for change.

The caterpillar doesn't emerge as a butterfly until the change is complete.

Sometimes I feel I'm in a state of constant change. Only concrete and statues have the intent of staying the same.

But, apparently, so do you.

Because every time I changed, you remained the same.

So now, one more thing must change.

My address.

Things that make the **heart feel insignificant:**

Knowing that it wasted time trying to create itself

into something it didn't think it was
into something it didn't think it could be
into something it had to pretend to be.

But then came the dreadfully painful moment –

when God showed it that everything
it was trying hard to be. . .

It already was.

Look Again (Men As Trees Walking)

I used to see men as trees walking –

they were majestic
and mighty
and tall

and as they walked, they loomed over me
because next to them I always felt small.

In the presence of these pines I would cower –

next to the cypress
the oak tree
and palm

their shadows cast a weight that covered me
only with weeds and bushes would I feel calm.

Intimidated by more than their size –

their sturdiness
their longevity
their pride

they accomplished great things with no effort
while all I did was pushed aside.

Then storm clouds came that tried to drown me –

the tsunami
typhoon
and hurricanes

as their waters absorbed within me
the stronger my roots became.

With stronger roots, I started really growing –

first a bud
then a sapling
then a tree

now there's one more man as a tree walking,
and that mighty sequoia is me.

The caterpillar doesn't go
inside its cocoon
until it's ready for change.

The caterpillar doesn't
emerge as a butterfly
until the change is complete.

"The Constant Metamorphosis"

From the Issues of My Heart, I Speak

Things that make the **heart feel staccato:**

Knowing each
        each memory brings
                brings feelings of
of misery and hope.

And even though
        though misery and hope are
                are two different ends
ends of the same spectrum, they

They both
        both reflect
                reflect and enunciate
        my memories of you.

Stutter.

I
I am
  at least I think
I am falling
falling in love
with you.

But, I
I am
conflicted, I am
because you –
you may
you may just love me, too.

But I am
scared, I am
hesitant, I am
to start
start down that path
that path again,

because the last
the last time I
I traversed that path,
my heart nearly
nearly drowned and quickly
had to learn how to swim.

But you -

yes, you -
you told me
that this time
my love need not fright,

because you,
once you start
start driving down
down the road called love
you don't want to stop at the first light.

Because love,
true love,
really true love,
is not just a thing to say.

Because love,
real love,
truly real love,
is something you practice every day.

Because love,
isn't love
until the word
becomes what you do,

and love,
doesn't equal life
until it inspires
the best parts of you.

Because you told me love,

true love,
really true love
doesn't require that you
love another.

But instead, love,
real love,
truly real love,
does require that you
love yourself.

So love,
my love,
my truly real love
is what I'm preparing
to surrender to you.

But if I do love,
your true love,
must be ready
to accept and share, too.

Because love,
please be sure love,
that it is love,
and not just like

because I want to love
to be free to love
and to climb with love
to higher heights.

So love,
I promise love
and that your love
is safe with me,

because love,
when I look at love
it shows your
reflection in me.

I just finally accepted it.
For myself.
For real this time. . .

Just come.

"The Invitation"

From the Issues of My Heart, I Speak

Things that make the **heart feel re-defined:**

Knowing that just yesterday, LOVE was just
another mis-defined, ordinary word.
Just another word like:
peace
quilt
napkin
contentment
cup
fork
harmony
rubber band, or
stapler . . .

Just ordinary.
But now, today, just today – LOVE was re-defined.

Be Still (Psalm 42)

Your quest was
  to capture my heart
but your conquest was my life

beyond the trials
  beyond the despair
    beyond the burdens and strife

Your love pushed past the barriers
It was apprehensive,
  but unafraid –

it knew the destination
  beyond the realm
was worth the scars the path made

Now my heart is healing
  from the scars born from its past

I see the scars as a celebration,
  they led me to love that will last

Now our lives are intertwining
  to be your hostage is my free will

your conquest paused my heart and mind
  now love, at last,

can stand still . . .
and know

that it has found God.

Because the truth is. . .
The whole truth is —
My heart is precious to me.
. . .
I've finally discovered its worth.
In doing so, I've also
discovered my own.

"Sentence Fragments"

From the Issues of My Heart, I Speak

Things that make the **heart feel educated:**

Knowing its dictionary has expanded –
It no longer just needs stale, trite, 4-letter words like:

Hate   Rage   Fury   Pain   Cold

Because now, the dictionary has doubled in size with
weightier, more optimistic words like:

Affectionate   Confident
Expressive   Demonstrative
Enthusiastic   Favorable
Meaningful   Purposeful
Significant   **Treasured**

And these words make the heart, and its dictionary,
feel so much better.

Increase my Vocabulary

Share with me a love
that increases my vocabulary
and not with negative words
like contention
    affliction
    disruption
  or concerned.

But share with me a positive love
that makes me acquiesce to my new vocabulary
with words like
I feel unencumbered
    uncluttered,
    unfettered,
  and unconfined.

It's no anomaly
that in a love that increases your vocabulary
that a sesquipedalian nature will arise.

So, to say something so tiny
as a simple "I love you"
can make big words evaporate like time.

And now two need a dictionary
to tread surreptitiously
through the magnitude of our love
        our words
    and their size.

For they each become gargantuan in nature
With each eruption in our hearts

As our small vocabulary
        small love
    and small thoughts
erode away.

Now reciprocity is real –

as real as our anticipation
as our minds and our hearts collide.

So, share with me a love,
one that is ever-evolving,
so that, with small words,
it can never be defined.

If this butterfly can cause the wind
And then flap against its flow,

Then, maybe,
Re-falling in love
won't be so bad,
Who knows where these
winds may blow?

"Going Against the Wind"

From the Issues of My Heart, I Speak

Things that make the **heart feel adventurous:**

When it learns the same lesson
countless others already have —

Where we look for God - -

Is often NOT the place where we find God.

Then its mind begins racing in anticipation
as it wonders. . .

Where will I "find" God today?!

Well Wishes

I used to wish and then worry a lot
and cast my pennies to the offering plate
in the same way I threw them into the wishing well –

with fingers crossed
in hopeful expectation

that God –
    or the wonderful wizard of Oz,
would magically make my worries disappear.

But,
just as Dorothy discovered,
neither Oz, nor God,
were the make-a-wish genies,
or wand-waving wizards,
or even the fix-every-problem handymen
we made them out to be.

God, not so much Oz, was so much more.

His mind was way beyond any
        wisdom I could conceive.

His scope far surpassed the
        wizarding world of Harry Potter

I mean –

Who needed three wishes
or a book of magic spells
when one miracle was more than enough
to change any circumstance?

Who needed a fairy godmother
to wave a wand and intervene
to basically recycle what I have for what I need
to turn my own pumpkins into a carriage with a steed
when God can wave a hand and create a whole world?

So I'm putting down my fairy tale books
and hopes in childish things
and picking up a new book from the shelf
one, I think, will be a great read!

It has tales of damsels in distress
And even some men who were in great need –
It has major feats like walking on water
And heroes who parted a sea.

It tells of mighty men who bowed to a baby
The world had yet to receive –

And there are tales of how great things can happen
- the only cost is to believe.

There are villains and adversaries
who constantly do dastardly things;
but, in this book, they're defeated each time
and now the reader has great victory.

But the greatest and the mightiest
and the most miraculous thing
is the love that flows within my heart
from each page I turn and read –

and how faith has replaced the pennies I brought
to the well for an offering
and how prayer has replaced the well wishes I made
to the wizard to be worry-free.

And the peace that the book said would surely come
really did surpass all understanding –

And now, it's no longer to Oz that I wish,
but to God, the One who changed me.

Things that make the **heart press pause**
(in life and on the cd or record player):

Aretha said,

"Hard, cold, and cruel
is the man
who paid
too much
for what he's got . . ."

And she was right —

Ain't no way.

The Narrative

It's funny how the mind can create a narrative
and tell a story of what's not there –
but the story's so real
that the heart can feel
the ointment for the scars it bears.

When the mind creates this narrative
the characters within seem real –
there was me and you
and my cousins too
and the warmth of the sun I could feel.

The warmth that came with the narrative
made we wish we could be there for years –
then a noise, loud and abrupt
caused me to wake up
and reality taunted, "I'm here. . ."

When reality doesn't match the narrative
the heart's often the last one to know –
true love wasn't there
because your heart wasn't fair
so either my hopes or my heart has to go.

Things that make the **heart feel manufactured:**

Knowing that, just like your
grandmother's patchwork quilts,

it was created from scraps of
worn,
torn,
and forlorn
pieces,

but the end result wasn't neglected . . .

it was priceless and

cherished.

The Mosaic

A mosaic is a collection
a collection of things once whole –
things, now, no longer useful,
remade with new purpose, restored.

It's a product of many broken pieces
like the hardened parts of liquid sand –
things once sculpted and found valuable,
in a variety of hues, shapes, and brands.

In life, we become mosaics
our memories the collections of things once known –
things that, somehow, have changed us,
the outcome of seeds we have sown.

I, too, am a mosaic
a collection of all who were here before –
a collection of all things deemed unworthy,
picked up from your trash left on the floor.

I'm a product of what you left broken
you couldn't deal so you left me behind –
forgotten, abandoned, and unspoken,
your actions weren't kind to my mind.

The pieces, whole, that now were broken,
I held them all like glue –
thought you would return to restore them,
but, that, you'd have to see value to do.

So I framed my heart in my mosaic

incased it with wood and glue –
thought, if you didn't see its value,
someone else should be able to.

But he only saw my brokenness
and played me into his hands –
he broke more of my broken pieces,
and ground my glass back to sand.

But I held tighter to my broken pieces
and guarded them with my life –
afraid to lose any piece of my shattered,
because my heart paid too high a price.

But love shouldn't leave you broken
and I didn't love me enough to say –
my mosaic and heart may be battered and torn,
but now, I'm finding the beauty in my pain.

If where love is, there is God
because God is love,
then where is God
if I don't love myself?

"Conjunctions and Contingencies"

From the Issues of My Heart, I Speak

Things that make the **heart feel regret:**

When it realizes it didn't listen
to the advice of the elders —

Believe a person when they *show* you who they are

and

Trust God enough to wait for what
He *tells* you He will do.

The Change Within the Cocoon

I came in as a hungry thing,
Ready to eat whatever the world fed me –

Trash, refuse, garbage, waste, nourishment, feces –

it didn't matter,
I ate it all.
I believed it all.
I got fat off it all.

All the time.

But life got to be too heavy,
so I climbed up a tree to die.

I wrapped myself up,
I hung a noose around the tree,

But rather than contracting around my neck,
it suspended my body in mid-air.

It pressed pause on my life as I knew it.
Suspended –
Not re-wound or fast-forwarded.
Paused –

But then came the change.
The change within the cocoon.
And when God pressed play,
I was made entirely new.

Things that make the **heart feel foolish:**

When the heart has been
looking for a home . . .

Outside of itself

but never looked within . . .

Where it biologically belongs.

Untitled (Inside Love)

I am
  encompassed
    encased
      embodied
and embraced.

I am
  boxed-in
  and sealed,
    surrounded by
    and concealed.

I am
  not beyond
  within reach
  solicited
  and beseeched.

I am
  invoked
    and entreated

I am
  sought after
  and needed.

I am
in
side

Love.

Things that make the **heart feel unashamed:**

When it can finally be

at peace with

and, actually, proud of

its scars - - -

because they show . . .

"I survived."

The Precipice

I'm standing at the precipice,
trying to decide what I should do –

and,
unlike before,
everywhere I look,
now –

 I see God.

I collided head on with destiny,
which caused me to face my fears.

Everything I sought to avoid,
now, is standing right here.

I swerved,
I veered,
I turned,
I swayed.

I swatted,
I squatted,
I ducked,
I waved.

I slid,
I hid,
I ran,
I cried –

And still from this date with destiny,

I could not hide.

I blamed others,
I became depressed –
Depression is a viable excuse
when you're a mess.

I self-sabotaged,
I turned to go back,
I gave my stuff away
so that I could lack.

But –

Despite all that left me,
God caused it to return –

He said, "From these life lessons,
you are going to learn;
though it did hurt,
your destiny won't burn.

While you may have scars,
you'll yet celebrate your wounds;
The scars serve as your reminder,
you survived what should have been your doom."

So, as I stand at this precipice
I look down into the sand,
I see some footsteps coming my way,
And a nail-scarred, outstretched hand.

I hear a voice that bids me,
"Come, my child, and see –

Because while you yet stand at this precipice, know you're standing here with me."

Things that make the **heart feel contaminated:**

When it feels it has

- subtracted

so much from itself,
that it feels it has nothing left to be an

+ addition

to someone else.

Live Love, Live

There will be no love dying here –

It won't need a band-aid
nor stitches,
No tourniquets,
nor gauze,
No defibrillators
nor life support.
No one will need to call the time of death
nor the next of kin.

This love needs no insurance to cover all its costs,
Its assurance rests in knowing this love will not be lost.
It's covered,
its sealed,
it's encompassed
and protected;

It's me, you, and God
Our trinity is connected

So you can put away the shovels,
The tractors, and bulldozer blades
No funeral will take place today –
There's no need to dig a grave.

But you can dig a deep flower bed
Because we're expanding our roots
As our love continues to thrive
It will produce many good fruits.

The ambulance can stay away,
No need to call 911 –
because this love will be here to stay,
Until our days are done.

I am
sought after
and needed.

I am
in
side

Love.

"Untitled (Inside Love)"

From the Issues of My Heart, I Speak

Things that make the **heart feel disenfranchised:**

Knowing that it doesn't own any
real estate
or stocks
or bonds
in your heart - - -

it barely has a mailbox.

Then it realizes . . .

it barely has a mailbox of its own.

Out of Character

I looked in the mirror
and I didn't recognize me,
I didn't recognize the eyes
I looked into the mirror to see.

I didn't recognize the face
that was right in front of mine,
so I turned around –
and looked again
but had the same feeling each time.

Unaware and confused,
When did this become me?
When did I start having the characteristics?
That, in others, I always hated to see?

Then I had two questions,
and their answers I needed to learn –

Who was this person in the mirror?

And when will I return?

Things that make the **heart feel liberated:**

When it stopped trying to

      fight

what it was

      supposed to be

and started

      becoming.

Speak, Heart, Speak

From the issues of my heart,
flow the abundance of my life
flow the origins of my strife
flow weapons sharper than a knife.

From the issues of my heart
are the sum of days that made me cry
of loved ones who said goodbye
and left me screaming to God "why?!"

Within the issues of my heart
is everything I fear
and all things I hold dear
and a future not yet here.

Within the issues of my heart
Is the sum of each and every day
How God loved me every way
And how he caused my mouth to say

From the issues of my heart
I share what I really think –

From the issues of my heart, I speak.

Proverbs 27:19
Just as water mirrors your face,
so your face mirrors your heart.

As you read each page,
I hope,
within the words,
you found the reflection of your heart
because

oftentimes,
it's rare that we listen to it.

So please,

If your heart ever tells you

"I Can't Breathe"

Please
stop
and listen.

From the Issues of My Heart, I Speak

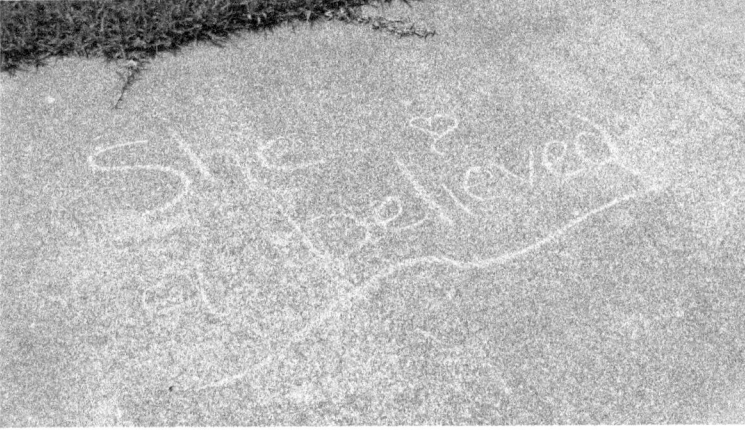

About the Author –

Sharon Session-Thomas is a native of Port Arthur, TX. As she grew up, her mother, Manda, was a math teacher and her father, Robert, was retired from the city sanitation department. Upon graduating from Abraham Lincoln High School, she went to Texas Christian University. There, she earned her Bachelors in English and Masters in Education. She is currently a teacher within her hometown school district. She and husband Jesse have one daughter, Averie.

Above all else, guard your heart because
from it, flow the issues of life.
Proverbs 4:23

www.ingramcontent.com/pod-product-compliance
Lightning Source LLC
Chambersburg PA
CBHW032007060426
42449CB00032B/1055